GENDER REJECTION©

GENDER REPLACEMENT

A DEVELOPMENTAL THEORY OF HOMOSEXUALITY

BY

J. SCOTT SINGMASTER M.S.

Gender Rejection / Gender Replacement: A Developmental Theory of Homosexuality

By J. Scott Singmaster M.S.   LLC

ISBN- 13: 9781479313945

ISBN-10 1479313947

Printed in the U.S.A.

Updated 07-15-19

Contents

Forward

1. It's not what you think
2. The Fine Line
3. Freud
4. The Stockholm Syndrome, Cognitive Dissonance & Codependency
5. Research/ Memories - Positive and Negative Reinforcement
6. Cover up & Restorative Therapy
7. Mother-infant Bonding
8. Illustrations
9. Identity
10. Now what?
11. Healing
12. A Message to Moms
13. Random thoughts
14. Jesus and You, a Love Story
15. The Beach Road
16. Conclusion

References

Forward

The purpose of writing this book is to introduce this theory called Gender Rejection and to discuss how a LGBT mind set and behavior can form within certain family dynamics. This is a *kind*, systematic, mechanistic, connect-the-dots description of how the thought process of a transgender individual may develop. For the most part, I want to take the focus off of the transgender individual and place it squarely on *generational family dynamics*.

It is not my intention to put down or condemn those who live an alternative life style in any way, shape or form, what-so-ever. I am *not* against anyone. I am not homo-phobic. I do not have a secret agenda. It is not my intention to bring harm to anyone or to throw anyone "under the bus." I will probably step on some toes though, but ultimately my hope is to bring light, truth and understanding to a confusing issue.

This information is directed toward those who are searching and who may feel that they have a double mind set, "Am I gay or not," and would like to possibly know why they think this way and it is also directed towards parents of a transgender individual. I use the terms gay, homosexual, gender dysphoria and transgender interchangeably.

This theory is easily applied and you can quickly see if it fits your life situation or someone's that you know. This theory probably does not apply to those who have been sexually abused, molested or violated in such a manner that has caused a homosexual orientation; however, you can gain other insight here that may help you understand your personal situation. This is not a "one size fits all" theory but I believe it will address a large percentage of those who face this issue.

This is a *generational issue* spanning *at least 3 generations* and probably more. An *abusive* grandparent, or other adult figure, (male or female) can produce a daughter who develops fear and unforgiveness issues. (The abuse can be *observed* within the family as well, i.e. dad is a wife beater). Because of a woman's unresolved issues with men or women, she in turn does not emotionally nurture the gender identity of her child, the gender that offended her, and because of this, a transgender mind set may develop in her child. The whole process begins with abuse, which leads to fear, which leads to *disarming or disassembling* a child's gender identity because it is perceived as harmful, fearful and unwanted. The Gender Rejection is generally targeted toward one child of a particular sex, although I have seen a gay son and daughter in the same family.

For the transgender individual, the issue is a coping mechanism and an adaptation to expectation. It is not just the rejection of their gender that children are responding to, it may also be to shame and guilt that they may feel for not being what "they are supposed to be." Shame is a powerful feeling and force, it reaches to the core of a person and affects an individual's very identity, their self-worth, who they actually are in their own minds. The Bible says, "As a man thinks, so is he." (Proverbs 23:7).

My heart goes out to those who are transgender or gay. I sincerely believe that the individual who has this belief about themselves has experienced rejection from key people, on many levels, over their entire life. I believe the whole issue is about how another person perceives a child's gender and that it has *nothing* to do with the child as a person and *everything* to do with another person's perception of that gender. I believe *gender approval* and affirmation is what the gay person has had withheld from them and this has caused cognitive and behavioral adjustments and directed them, so to speak, to comply with someone else's personal beliefs. Again, it all begins as a generational issue founded in abuse, fear and ultimately a form rejection.

I am not going to "thump the Bible" but I do mention God in this book because I believe that He is the author and creator of life, and that He wants you to know who He is and who you are. God is love and love is patient and kind so *God is patient and kind.* (1 Corinthians 13) We can trust and rely in His goodness to bring us to a place of peace and wholeness. It is usually the relationships that we have with those around us that help define "who we are," but we also have to look to God. He is our creator and He has created us for a purpose. He is our father. He created us to have a relationship with Him. For this reason, it is so important to read the Bible to see what God says about Himself and us as well. I will include a small chapter later in this book to cover some of His thoughts toward you.

"From birth I was cast upon you, from my mother's womb, you have been my God."

- Psalm 22:10

1

CHAPTER ONE

It's Not What You Think

Not everyone understands homosexuality, but *everyone* understands rejection. I believe that homosexuality is rooted in rejection, but it is not the type of rejection that some may think. I used to think that a male who gravitated toward another male was looking for something that was denied to him in his relationship with his dad. (That may seem naïve but that is how it appeared to me). It is possible that his dad was too rejecting, too busy or somehow abandoned his son, but I propose that that is not what the rejection is. I propose that the rejection is actually rejection of the child's sexuality, more specifically their *gender identity*, by the mother or Primary Emotional Caregiver ©. I propose that she is the Gender Rejecter, however, <u>unknowingly</u>. I believe the entire process is taking place on a subconscious level for both the mother and the child. This does *not* mean that a mother does not love her child. What it may mean is that she has unresolved issues with those of a particular gender and these repressed thoughts, feelings and emotions are translated into the rejection of a child's gender because of what *"that gender"* represents to the mother.

As I mentioned, I always thought that the male was drawn toward another male to gain some lost element from his relationship with his dad, but now I see that the child is not drawn toward the same sex necessarily, but rather, because we are all sexual beings, they gravitate toward the same sex because their self-perception has been reversed and they have met someone who has a similar mind set.

This is what this theory looks like in action; a woman gives birth to a male child but because anger, bitterness and unforgiveness, due to abuse experienced by her or observed in her childhood, she now has severe, unresolved men issues, so the mother does not or cannot acknowledge the "male-ness" of the child. She does not encourage it, ("Mommy's big boy," etc.) she is emotionally distant and maybe even hostile. Children are extremely sensitive and if a child perceives this emotional distancing or *indifference* and discerns that mom doesn't "like me" the way that I was born, (maybe she is more open and loving toward a sister or other female companions), then the child will begin Gender Replacement and dis-robe their gender identity, alter their core perception of themselves and they will begin to deny their own sexuality and this is based on *fear of abandonment.* A child *needs* to have acceptance from their mother, if they do not receive gender identity affirmation, a child can reject and replace their own gender concept as a coping mechanism to an emotionally rejecting environment; they will side with the emotional attitude of their mother. After many years of a parent under-nurturing the gender identity of their child, the child's gender concept is now dismantled, and it leaves the child (now an adult) without the capacity to emotionally or mentally relate to the opposite sex, so the individual ends up congregating with others like themselves. Homosexuality then becomes a mindset with ensuing behaviors.

So, a male homosexual is created by the rejection of his gender/sexuality by his Primary Emotional Caregiver and that person is usually the mother. Regarding lesbians, it is the *same* process. When a mother, who has unresolved issues with women, has a daughter, she may not embrace and nurture the sexuality or gender identity of her child and the child may initiate Gender Replacement and act out the opposite role of how she was born so that she will be "acceptable" and loved by her mother. The child is demonstrating to her mom how "not female" she is. It is ultimately all about the daughter *not being female* in both of their perceptions.

Lesbianism is actually closer to the truth of the actual dynamic taking place between a mother and her child, but the motive for the behavior is what has remained unclear and that is where we need to focus. Ultimately, I propose that a lesbian is not practicing an alternative life style because she is attracted to the same sex, but rather her need is for her mom to accept her so she adopts this "new gender identity" over the span of her childhood. This adaptation is necessary because, for some reason, being female was unacceptable to mom and now the emotional motive for the child is to comply with expectations and/ or avoid rejection. I am sure the mother loves their child in these instances but again, I strongly believe there are subconscious, unresolved issues within the mother that are mutated into gender rejection attitudes and behaviors toward their daughter.

When a child is 0 – 3 years old I believe they are following cues for desired behaviors. When they get a little older, I believe they become more cognizant of their own sexuality, start to experience crushes and this is where conflicts begin to arise as they become aware of the duality of their affections. When they do become aware this may be the time where the individual behavior is more deliberately aligned with parental expectations because the "rewards" for acceptable behaviors are more noted and sought after.

Generally, there are three categories of rejecting behaviors that a mother can elicit.

- Anger, Fear, Unforgiveness, and Bitterness
- Apathy, Indifference, Ambivalence
- Over indulgence, Pampering

Although these attitudes seem very different, they each can in fact be an attitude or behavior that can be gender rejecting and thereby deeply affect a child's personal development.

Before a child can cognitively assess aspects of their relationship with their mother, I believe they are simply complying with expectations. Children act and respond by continuing to do behaviors that are rewarded with emotional nurturing and they let go of behaviors that are ignored or shunned. (Operant conditioning)

The process may unfold in this manner when the child is older (4 and up), they may notice they are being distanced in one way or another; fear may seep in. I believe subconsciously they identify what the issue is, *their* gender (and accompanying behavior) then a second stage begins and they feel shame for what they are. Finally, guilt is the third component in this whole process. Fear, guilt and shame become the compounding mix that initiates the whole Gender Replacement process and it is based on survival instincts because of feeling emotional isolation and having fear of abandonment. The child 'un-does' themselves gender-wise because of the stress of rejection and when the mom accepts the "new gender" and new behaviors, then the child feels relief. The child no longer behaves like they did and the new behavior is rewarded with nurturing and acceptance and it continues indefinitely. The whole process from the child's point of view could be a type of survival mechanism but I believe it is all subconscious, and the process is *extremely subtle* and *incremental*.

When these individuals are toddlers I believe they are simply complying with emotional and verbal cues on how they are expected to behave and they may not experience all of the internal emotional processes of overcoming rejection etc., because, after all, they are simply children and they are not necessarily unlearning anything in particular or making adjustments in thought or behavior regarding their sexuality; they may be simply following parental guidance, steps and cues. I also believe the personality of a child may be a factor. A "type -A" child, for example, may be able to rebuff negative attitudes and have a stronger sense of self, and a more compliant child may be the one who is more likely to adapt to expectations.

Mothers are our Primary Emotional Caregivers most of the time. They are our *emotional* survival person; our contact with life. If a child perceives that they are not receiving the love and recognition that they so desperately depend on, they will emotionally and mentally adapt to what is expected of them in order to get the love that they have to have. This is basically how we all learn to "behave" when we are growing up. A father can contribute to this process if he has issues with a gender but I believe his influence is a compounding factor rather than an instigating element.

What can be confusing about homosexuality and this theory is that the whole person is not rejected; rather, it is specifically *their gender identity*. It is compartmentalized rejection by the parent. The mother does love their child but what we may be seeing is a child that is adapting to a role that has been inferred by the mother and created and implemented by the child and then the mother re-enforces the new behavior with approval. The child has picked up on her subconscious and non-verbal vibes and is responding in such a way as to comply with expectations.

The effects of rejection can be tremendous, obvious and long lasting. The child receives subconscious emotional cues or vibes from the mom, and then he/she alters their own behavior. The child, in essence, convinces themselves that they are not how they were born; they change or adapt their mind-set, their self-perspective and adaptive behaviors, so that they can obtain love and maintain acceptance. Intimidation and bullying on an emotional level can also influence a child's behavior but this is a more extreme variation of this theory. (i.e. A child softens their speech and mannerisms so as to not be perceived as provoking, intimidating or confrontational.)

―――――――――――――――

The act of homosexuality is *not* the issue at hand; it is the tip of the iceberg. The act of homosexuality is merely one of several acts that are the final expression of a role that has been inadvertently imposed on a child due to Gender Rejection, combined with the child *themselves* rejecting and replacing their own gender as something wrong or something to be ashamed of or something that needs to change, thereby altering their persona and internal beliefs, choosing a third alternative, "I'm gay, I'm the opposite of how I was born," and all of this is to accommodate an unaccepting parent. Again, the whole process is probably based in shame for how they were born, coupled with guilt for being who they are and it is finally combined with fear of isolation, abandonment and emotional distancing. A young child may simply be experiencing operant conditioning where the parent nurtures and rewards the behaviors of the child that they want to see and they shun the child's natural behaviors. Based on the child's age there seem to be two "forces" at work influencing the child's behavior, internal and external. Ultimately though, children want to comply with expectations.

Recently I had a friend tell me that his 7-year-old son started saying things like, "I want to be a girl daddy." The son would also say the same things to my friend's wife and she would say things like, "no, when you get older, you're going to meet a nice girl and have a family…" My friend also told me he would redirect his son's thinking with reminders of girls that he had expressed interest in but the child would still say similar things from time to time. After I started writing this book my friend's wife, unbeknownst to me, took this information that I had shared with them and sat down with her son one night and told him how *she* had prayed and wanted a <u>boy</u> and that he was the <u>boy</u> that she always wanted and that <u>he</u> was a gift from God." Well my buddy said to me one day, "Remember how our son would say such and such about being a girl?" I said "yes." He then said, "We noticed that he has stopped saying it." He then told me what had happened. He said, "We tried to *redirect* his speech and thoughts, by me, a male, and by my wife, a female, and nothing changed... What our son responded to was *affirmation and acceptance* of how he was *created (physiologically)* and how God had made him and that was how *she wanted him*." As it turns out, it was <u>acceptance by his *mother,*</u> not redirection by either of them, that made all the difference. (I had actually finished writing this book but when heard this story and I had to do a re-write to include it because it demonstrated this theory so well).

It is extremely important to emphasize *that moms and dads are people too* and the whole process of the creation of a person who is transgender is very subconscious and very subtle. It would be unwise to go on a tirade against anyone because their attitudes toward your gender were un-nurturing. *I strongly recommend family counseling* along the lines of this theory if you believe this dynamic may have taken place in your family. It is important to understand that parents have their own pain and now that you are aware of the possible roots of your pain and confusion, what needs to be done is to begin praying and ask God to start bringing healing and understanding and *forgiveness* to everyone involved.

If this theory applies to you or someone you know, please understand, it is an issue of gender rather that sex. It is about how you were created, not about what you do. It is about your core identity, not about your actions. It is about your need for acceptance by someone who should have loved and nurtured you for exactly how you were created, male or female.

I remember a guy in high school who was gay and I recall him saying that he believed his mom was probably gay as well. One generation does influence the next so to see this theory more clearly; one must look back, one to two generations, to find the pattern of beliefs and attitudes of the mother, and her parents, toward each of the genders. Any presence of abuse or observation of abuse in the mom's past is *the red flag* to look for along with present attitudes of indifference, jealousy or competitiveness towards either gender.

I know two individuals whose moms tried to overtly change their gender orientation by saying things like, "she hates men" to family members as if to instill a new mind set. The other individual was male and his mom would yell at him, "you're gay, you're gay!" but neither of them became gay because what was missing was the nurturing reward to change. These two examples are overt attempts to deviate a child their natural course but in most instances the process is subconscious. The child must receive positive affirmations to make the change.

To the person with an LGBT mindset I say, this issue is *incrementally* integrated into one's psyche and I propose that *you are not gay,* but rather, it is your gender that was rejected and that you may have rejected your own gender as well. You have the physiology of a particular gender; the confusion is your mind-set which was formed by disapproval or rejection.

Occasionally I have heard the argument that people cannot come out of an alternative life style because that would mean that they were not being true to their real selves and that it would be a type of brain washing, but what we need to understand is that is *exactly* what has happened in the first place. We are all born with a particular gender, but it is possible for a parent to not accept their child's gender and deny them proper nurturing and acceptance. If this happens the child will make the necessary adjustments within themselves, emotionally, behaviorally and physically (through clothing and surgery later in life, for example), and transition into what is needed to get the love that all children must have. The whole process is an adaptive, coping behavior to a perceived "life threatening" or emotionally distressing situation. (Again, it is possible the child is simply following cues and vibes from a parent regarding expected behavior.)

Behavior

We see evidence of Gender Replacement when you observe behavior. Generally, although not always, the gay male is more effeminate acting and the girls act more masculine. I propose that a *role* has been adopted because subconscious motives are present prompting them to act in such a way as *to be the opposite* of what their mom disdained. If you notice, adult homosexual men seem to gravitate toward women. I propose that this is because they are still seeking nurturing from women in general and many times these women feel less threatened by this type of male so the relationship is self-perpetuating; The male is nurtured by the relationship with the female and this reinforces his behavior. The effeminate behavior is to be disarming toward women because that is the *original interaction dynamic that was established with their mothers.*

It's all about the individual's relationship with women. I believe most of their behaviors are learned behaviors. These behaviors can be addressed when one understands the foundational beliefs that were laid and that when these *lies of rejection* are confronted one by one, the truth about who an individual really is can replace incorrect mindsets that have long been in in place. (The Truth will set you free. John 8:32)

While growing up I knew an individual who most in our group new "was gay" but he would act gay sometimes and other times he would not. It appeared to be a choice, and at the very least, an expression of an internal conflict.

Regarding those who cross dress, I suspect that men who wear any type of ladies' garments are not trying to be a girl, rather, they like how they *feel* when they wear the clothes. It's not that they want to be a woman; it's that they want to feel nurtured by something feminine. All the behaviors under this theory are adaptive thinking and adaptive behaviors to feel better, to feel nurtured, to feel loved and to be accepted.

2

CHAPTER TWO

The Fine Line

Although I did not personally struggle with the issue of homosexuality, based on *this* theory of Gender Rejection, I understand it… it could have happened to me.

My mom was sexually abused by her father and he had been abused by a female caretaker after his mom had died in child birth. Because of my mom's abuse she developed obvious problems in her relationships with men. She had severe unresolved issues.

Because of this there were distinct times when the internal conflicts of her feelings toward men would surface. Ninety eight percent of the time she was a good and nurturing mom but there were a few incidences when she wasn't and I will share those here to help illustrate my point.

One day when I was about 4 or 5 years old, I was sitting on the couch with my mom and there was a space between us and I kept pushing a toy airplane toward her and she kept pushing it back at me. (She was trying to read a magazine). The airplane was one of those dye-cast metal toys like you see Match-Box Cars® made out of and it was about 5 inches across. So, I kept pushing it because I thought we were playing a game. The next thing I know my head felt numb and I was disoriented. I then felt something wet near the corner of my eye so I reached up and touch it and I realized that it was blood. What had happened was she had grabbed the airplane and hit me in the head with it and the wing had cut my brow. Then I said, "I'm bleeding." (Internally I knew this would change the tone of the moment because mom was a good mom if there was a crisis). She then rushed me into the bathroom. My dad was in the house too, although not present during the incident, and I remember them tending to my wound and I also remember her saying to my dad that she "threw the plane and it bounced off the couch and hit me" as if it was an accident.

She was also abusive with discipline at times. She could wield a belt in such a way that it would make Indiana Jones and his bull whip look like a novice. I am not saying that there were not times that I deserved punishment, but I do remember occasions in which I was confused as to why I was "getting it." I also decided at one point in my life that I would not continue this type of punishment on my kids.

My mom's perception of men was tainted. She thought people like Michael Jackson, for example, were the ideal male. After my parents divorced, she had a few gay men friends (they were less threatening) but unfortunately the men that she did date were substandard. One in particular was in and out of mental institutions the whole time they dated. She was a rescuer in this case and it put her in more of a position of helper/ controller, rather than at the *perceived mercy* of a healthy male companion. She had normal attractions to men as a whole but her ability to form healthy relationships was severely lacking. She had a conflict; she liked men, but she feared and distrusted them too. There were moments when her conflicts were apparent. I thank God that the moments were few as I mentioned before, because I, who basically have a compliant personality, could have easily gone along with whatever was "expected of me."

To my mom's credit she was very creative, however, one time, when I was in the third grade and the Christmas season was approaching, she decided to "decorate me" for school and she tied silver jingle bells to my pristine white sneakers and ushered me into the holiday season. So, there I was, 8 years old, jumping around school sounding like Rudolph The Red Nosed Reindeer minus the red nose. I became acutely aware of my different "décor" when we were asked by the teacher to walk quietly from the library back to class...yeah, not so much...Rudolph here was "jingling all the way." It was then that I realized nobody else's mom decorated them with adorning jingle bells or Christmas cheer and when I got back to my desk, I quickly took them off and tossed them into the trash. (Free at last). This incident along with another when I was 10, were distinct moments when I consciously remembered making my own choice about compliance to expectations.

When I was ten years old, we went on a family vacation to Massachusetts to visit my cousins. My cousins lived right on a lake which was the coolest thing possible to a ten-year-old boy who was practically born with a fishing pole in his hand. The year was 1974. The hit song that summer was, The Night Chicago Died, by the British group, Paper Lace; I think they played it every hour. Little did I know, though, this would be the summer of a new discovery...*girls*!

Next to my cousin's house there were two summer homes and there happened to be a family vacationing in one of them and that's when I met my cousin's friend, Annette. I was 10, she was 12 and life took on new meaning. Our friendship was immediate. We were like Kevin and Winney from the Wonder Years. I remember distinctly counting down the days until my family had to leave. I remember being clearly conscious of day 10...10 days left... an eternity in some respects, but with the end speedily approaching. I was in love now and *time* was my enemy.

After a few days of walking on air, my cousin and my sister ratted me out to my mom that I was "seeing someone." Not that it was a secret, but it is not something that you run home and tell your mother. So, there they were, in my aunt's kitchen; my sister…cousin…mother and aunt, and here I come walking in (on cue), while the "kin folk" were spilling *my beans* and my mom turns to me and *bellows,* …"HOW'S ANNETTE?!?!"

GEEEZ MOM!! COULD YOU SAY IT ANY LOUDER, I DON'T THINK MICHIGAN HEARD YOU!!??...was my internal response, along with… "BAGGED!!"

I don't think there is a greater wet blanket than to hear your mom say your girlfriends name out loud….I think it's only surpassed by the question, "How's your little girl friend?"… (Ewe)

Well the cat was out of the bag and I responded with a sheepish, "good." Then she said, "I guess I'll have to share a part of you now?" Honestly, a feeling of dread hit me at that moment. I think somehow, I knew that a separation was needed. I felt almost smothered and held back and this was my clear opportunity to make some sort of break…

… "Nope…*all of me*," was my response.

Later that night she recanted the conversation and commented to me that it was a "very mature thing that I had said," and I could tell that she respected it…. My mom did an amazing thing that day. She acknowledged my individuality as a young <u>man</u>. I was released to date!!! (Just kidding, I was only 10) But a great foundation was laid that day; A new realm of my feelings, thoughts and desires emerged that summer and they were acknowledged, even accepted.

Fast forward a few years and we can see an attitude change in my mom. My parents have gone through a divorce by this point and we had moved to New Hampshire. My mom was still fairly neutral about my maturity and growth as I became a young man but there was a certain vibe that started to creep in. Although she would happily take me to events like high school dances and nothing about it was discouraged, she began to envision me going into seminary. We had started to attend church regularly and I did feel a particular closeness to God and the idea of me being a priest became more conversational as time went on. Her attitude toward the idea was strong, though, and I was just trying it out as a new idea. We were not church goers up until that point so going to a Catholic church was a whole new experience. Along with us going to church and me toying with the idea of being a priest, I could not help but also feel another "vibe" from her and this was confirmed after my first year in college.

I had come home from my freshman year and I found myself in a very painful situation. As my mom and sister and myself were all sitting at the kitchen table, I started to get all choked up because of some really bad news that I needed to share and I was so emotional that I could not get any of the words out so my mom decided to help me and she blurted out, "ARE YOU GAY?!" Well that changed the tone of the moment long enough for me to say, (along with my sister), "NO MOM…my *girlfriend* has a brain tumor." So, there it was…my mom's expectation for me was to be a gay priest. I think she thought that college life would have somehow brought out whatever she thought was in me (or her repressed hope) and that this was my "coming out" speech... Sigh… There was a second time that she said exactly the same thing so it was more than apparent that this was on her mind. I think she wanted an "in" with God by having a priest in the family and to also have a non-threatening, non-traditional male as well.

She would do other small things too that in retrospect were a little bit conflicting. She would sometimes buy me clothes that were too flamboyant. I remember a coat she bought me one time, it had big patches of red, yellow, and blue. It reminded me of The Partridge Family bus. I was already 22 at that point with dark hair and a beard it just did not quite "fit." As a kid I remember purple pants at Easter time, white sneakers, yellow pajamas, etc.... There were not a lot of signs of her internal conflict but when I look back, I can see a few.

Today I serve God as a father and as a husband and with general church involvement and my life is fulfilled; this is what I was created for but I think one can get a small glimpse here as to how someone else (especially a parent or authority figure) can influence an individual to go a different way.

(The girlfriend lived by the way)

3

CHAPTER THREE

Freud

When one looks at early world maps that were created by explorers such as Columbus, Magellan, Ponce De Leon and others, you can see that, they are pretty accurate, albeit a bit distorted. However, no one looks back and scoffs at them for not getting it right; after all, they were pioneers, explorers, doing what no one else had ever done before.

One such pioneer in his field was Sigmund Freud. Today, many look at his early theories, as he tried to map the mind and emotions, and they do scoff at him. In light of newer evidence, some of his viewpoints may seem misguided at best and bizarre at worst; however, no one doubts that he is considered the father of modern psychology and psychoanalysis to be more specific.

Freud did a study of one homosexual woman and he followed her life for a few years and he made some very interesting notations. Having read them, I found some things that were very intriguing. It seems he had observed and noted several puzzle pieces of my theory but he did *not* incorporate them as part of his theory.

In Freud's book, <u>Sigmund Freud: Sexuality and the Psychology of Love</u>, He makes several statements regarding a mother's attitude of her young, eighteen-year-old daughter, who is a practicing homosexual. Many of his statements of observation epitomize my theory. I will list the statements chronologically:

> "The mother's attitude towards the girl was not easy to grasp. She (the mother) was still a youngish woman, who was evidently *unwilling to relinquish* her own claim to find favor by means of her beauty. All that was clear was that *she did not take her daughter's passion so tragically* as did the father

nor was she so incensed at it. She had even for a long time *enjoyed her daughter's confidence* concerning the love-affair and her opposition seemed to have been aroused mainly by the harmful publicity with which the girl displayed her feelings. She (the mother) had herself suffered from some *neurotic troubles* and enjoyed a great deal of consideration from her husband; she was quite *unfair in her treatment of her children*, decidedly *harsh* toward her daughter and *overindulgent* toward her three sons, the youngest of whom had been born after a long interval and was then not yet three years old."

So, the mother was still young and did not make a place for her daughters' beauty, there may have been *competition* which would have stifled the natural growth and maturity of the daughter's sexuality. The mother was *not upset* over the affair, because it suited her emotional motives I suspect. She bonded with her daughter over the topic, so there is a *type* of closeness which would have been nurturing and therefore rewarding to the daughter. Freud said the mom was neurotic and implied that she was emotionally dependent on the husband, so there was some other issue going on at home as well. And finally, the mom treated her boys well and was harsh to the daughter. It was right after the birth of the third boy that her homosexuality became extremely apparent.

Based on my theory, I believe the girl felt rejected by the mom. The mom favored the boys and was harsh toward her. When the girl's homosexuality intensified after the birth of the third boy, they continued their mother daughter bonding time and confidences were shared and the mother's disapproval was absent. (Notice the pattern.) I think the birth of a third male child for the mother to dote over caused the girl to "snap" and go head long into an alternative life style. (There were earlier signs as well)

> In Regards to the love interest of the 18-year-old, Freud writes, "She had thus not only chosen a feminine love-object, but had also developed a *masculine attitude* towards this object."

I propose the more masculine attitude is to put more distance emotionally and mentally between herself and her true gender, the wider the distance, the more her relationship with her mother is emotionally rewarded because she has demonstrated greater Gender Replacement.

When this girl was approximately 13 or 14, Freud states,
she developed a tender and according to general opinion, an *exaggeratedly strong affection* for a small boy, not quite three years old, whom she used to see regularly at the playground in one of the parks. She took to the child so warmly that in consequence a permanent friendship grew up between her and his parents. One may infer from this episode that at the time, she possessed of a strong desire to be a mother herself and to have a child. However, after a short time she grew *indifferent* to the boy and began to take an interest in mature, but still youthful, women; the manifestations soon led her father to administer a mortifying chastisement to her.

I infer, on the other hand, that she had a void in her life. She had watched her mother doting on her brothers and I propose that because she had observed her mother's apparent fulfillment in a relationship with her sons, rather than with a daughter, so she, for a short time, tried it herself but soon realized that her relationship with this small boy did not provide the fulfillment that she had hoped for.

Freud writes,

> The latter (the mother) still youthful herself, saw in her rapidly developing daughter an inconvenient competitor; she favored the sons at her expense, limited her independence as much as possible and kept an especially strict watch against any close relation between the girl and her father.

I think the mother clearly has women issues and in-turn discouraged the daughter from being herself and from becoming a woman. She interfered with any normal male female exchange that could be learned from time spent with her dad as well. I propose the girl needed love and attention from her mother, as any normal child would, and when she perceived that she was not receiving it she began Gender Replacement to maintain her mother's affection as best she could.

Freud goes on to say in that paragraph,

> A yearning from the beginning for a kinder mother would, therefore, have been quite intelligible

(INDEED), but why it (the homosexual behavior) should have flamed up just then and in the form of a consuming passion is not comprehensible.

I believe what happened was that the daughter had wanted a relationship with her mother but her mother made noted efforts to thwart that and at the birth of a third brother (whom the mother doted over) the daughter was at a breaking point and she made an all-out effort to gain the attention of the mother, *which she did achieve*, by pursuing women and not men.

This was Freud's analysis:

> The girl was just experiencing the revival of the infantile Oedipus-complex at puberty when she suffered a great disappointment. She became keenly conscious of the wish to have a child, and a male one; that it was her father's child and his image that she desired, her consciousness was not allowed to know. And then-it was not she who bore the child, but the unconsciously hated rival, her mother. Furiously resentful and embittered, she

turned away from her father and from men altogether. After this first great reverse she forswore her womanhood and sought another goal for her libido.

I can sort of see Freud's line of thinking here but I think he makes way too many assumptions about improvable motives. My conclusions are based on behavior that is observable with a guess at *only one motive* and that is that the child wanted to be loved. Freud made great notations about her life but he did not connect the dots in the manner that do which I believe tells a much clearer and simpler story.

> After her disappointment, therefore, this girl had entirely repudiated her wish for a child, the love of a man, and womanhood altogether. *(The Gender Replacement was complet*e). Now it is evident that at this point the developments open to her were very manifold; what actually happened was the most extreme one possible. She changed into a man and took her mother in place of her father as her love-object. Her relation to her mother had certainly been *ambivalent* from the beginning and it proved

easy to revive her earlier love for her mother (*Now confident in her changed life-style I propose*) and with its help to bring about an over-compensation for her current hostility towards her. Since there is little to be done with the real mother, there arose from the conversion of feeling described, the search for a mother-substitute to whom she could become passionately attached.

Freud's conclusion is close to my theory, however, I say it is *not* the pursuit of the other woman as a substitute for the mother, as he states, but rather a substitute *for a man,* because now the girl is acting the role of a man and *men seek women* and that is the inadvertent end result because of the gender rejecting attitudes of her mother. I continue to propose that the girl is not looking for an intimate relationship with her mom or dad, but rather, she wants parental affirmation for her true gender identity which she was not receiving.

In this family dynamic, jealousy may be the motivating factor that causes the mother to shun the woman-hood of her daughter so that there would be no competition. (As if they were in the same arena anyway) Either way, the affect is the same, the daughter under goes Gender Replacement, and the mother gets her desire and the daughter gets a form of approval. This is shown clearly in the next excerpt.

> In her actual relations with her mother there was a practical motive furthering the change of feeling which might be called an "advantage through illness." The mother herself still attached great value to the attentions and the admiration of men. If, then, the girl became homosexual and left men to her mother (in other words, "retired in favor of" the mother), she removed something which had hitherto been partly responsible for her mother's disfavor. (*I say she got out of the way to please mom and gain approval and avoid emotional abandonment. This is probably the true motivation for the daughter to change.*)

That paragraph may contain the entire issue. The mom had women issues and because of jealousy, she therefore passively aggressively under nurtures her daughter and the daughter never fully becomes the women she was created to be.

...It was remarkable, by the way that both parents behaved as though they understood the secret psychology of their daughter. The mother was tolerant as though she appreciated the favor of her daughter's "retirement" from the arena; the father was furious, as though he realized the deliberate revenge directed against him by his wife.

I propose that there was a serious dysfunctional family dynamic taking place. The mother seemed to be a classic narcissist and possibly histrionic. I base this on Freud's statement that described her as neurotic. Also, the girl may have indeed been directing revenge at her dad for not putting an end to the mother's shenanigans in the way she raised and treated her verses her brothers. The father may have been too passive as well. It sounds like mom was a very unhealthy center of the family. She had her husband tending to her "*with considerations,*" as Freud mentioned, she seemed to still need the attention of men, which I surmise ticked off her husband and she had three sons on whom she doted for possible reciprocal admiration. Never-the-less, it's the daughter who pays the price of confused sexual orientation because of a distinct lack of affection and approval by her mother and a division placed by the mother which caused a distant father.

It would not surprise me to learn that one or more of her brothers became a homosexual due to the mother's strong bonding with them, she could easily withhold *gender approval©* and get them to stay as 'mama's boys,' rather than let them marry and become men with families etc. Since the mother also seemed to have men issues, such as still wanting their admiration after she was already married with four kids, plus being unkind to the dad by putting a division between him and his daughter, based on my theory, I could easily see more homosexuality developing in this family.

The confusion of what we observe verses what we understand can lie in the fact that the mother appears to be affectionate, even overly so with the brothers, but I suggest it can be *overcompensation because of men hating issues.* I think that there is sufficient evidence that the mother has issues with *both genders.*

(When I was younger, I met a brother and sister while on a camping weekend. He was gay and she was a lesbian. I remember thinking at the time, "what kind of family dynamic is going on in their house hold that they would produce *two* kids that are gay?" Today I would speculate that their mom had severe unresolved issues with both genders.)

At one point, Freud's patient attempted suicide, which comes as no surprise. The tension of the conscious and unconscious desires of her parents must have been exasperating. Freud said it happened immediately after her father saw her walking with her "lady friend" and she then flung herself over a railing and fell. Suicide is a call for help and if her dad was the last family member to see her, I suspect she was "calling out to him."

Transference may be occurring in the dysfunction of their family. It is possible that, although the girl longed for the affection and approval of her mom, that she hated her at the same time for withholding it. Instead of hating what she wanted to love and be loved by (her mom), she then transferred the hatred to her dad. The mom had set up a division anyway so why not? This duality of emotions of needing love and hating her mom is what I suspect fueled the angry rift between her and her dad, and that these "feelings" towards dad were not necessarily her own idea. I say this because the only evidence of division mentioned is the father's fury over the homosexuality, other than that there is no other mention of any incidents that caused an issue.

I think the daughter was following cues from her mom that said, "This is the way we treat daddy," and maybe all men. I speculate that her angering him with her affairs may have doubled as an attention seeking behavior simply because of his overall lack of attention and involvement. Maybe she was just carrying out her "duty" to be hostile to dad. Or maybe she was trying to get her dad to "man up" since she did attempt suicide right after seeing him.

(Also, if it pleased the mother that the daughter was bitter toward the dad, then that would be one more issue that she and her mom could bond over.)

Freud made one statement regarding homosexual men which was, "homosexual men have experienced an especially strong fixation in regard to the mother..." I postulate that the male is fixated with the mother because he has not received the *correct* affirmation that he needs and longs for, not really knowing that that is what he is even longing for.

I have observed women in single parent households, (my mom included) who do over confide and lean on their sons and it is emotionally inappropriate. The mother is discussing life situations that are too overwhelming for her and forcing the child to emotionally bear some of the load when the child simply does not have the capacity to do so. This can cause immaturity, (I know from my own life) as well as an emotionally enmeshed bond between mother and son that inhibits his normal emotional growth.

One behavior that can easily be misunderstood and misconstrued as loving is *over indulgence* and *pampering* of a male child. This causes immaturity and an unhealthy emotional enmeshment because normal demands are not placed on the child at different age levels and "mommy takes care of everything," thereby causing the child to lean way too much on their mother in emotional ways, rather than start to become more manly and emotionally independent.

To even begin to remedy this situation, and address how a LGBT mindset occurs, it necessitates that a parent explains the dynamics that may have taken place in their relationship, *and take responsibility for it.* The parent needs to set the record straight so that the child knows the facts about how they were raised versus how they should have been raised.

CHAPTER FOUR

The Stockholm Syndrome, Cognitive Dissonance & Codependence

Although the following example may be a bit extreme regarding the development of homosexuality, there are some distinct elements that should be paid attention to.

Thanks to Hollywood, the Stockholm syndrome has become well known but it was recognized before in studies of hostage and *abusive situations*. It was originally defined by psychiatrist Frank Ochberg to aid the management of hostage situations.

The Stockholm syndrome occurs when a captive is isolated and threatened with death, but receives acts of kindness by the captor. It usually takes three or four days for the psychological shift to manifest itself.

In these situations, the *captive* becomes very focused on the needs of the captor, avoiding anything that is perceived to "set them off." Because of the intensity of focus, the captive becomes enmeshed in the captor's emotional state, which builds empathy and a type of bonding takes place.

Four elements need to occur in the captive relationship for this syndrome to take place:
1st, a threat to one's physical or psychological survival and the belief that the abuser would carry out the threat.

2nd, small kindnesses from the abuser.

3rd, isolation from perspectives other than those of the abuser.

4th, the perceived inability to escape the situation.

I would translate these 4 conditions as:

1. The fear of abandonment or isolation.
2. The child's material needs are met.

3. There is no parent of the opposite sex or other role model to balance or rebuff negative influences.
4. The child has nowhere else to go.

Along with the Stockholm syndrome there is another psychological phenomenon that could explain my theory even more; here it is about adults, but imagine it is about a child.

Cognitive Dissonance, in general, is the reason people change their beliefs. In theory, there are two sets of thoughts or belief's that are opposite, they are incongruent; the thoughts do not line up between two people or situations; What we believe is conflicting with what is communicated to us and that makes a situation *emotionally uncomfortable*. Cognitive Dissonance, or "the gap" between conflicting information, can be reduced by *adding new thoughts and attitudes*. (i.e. I am not a male/female; I am something else) rationalizing and justifying may be part of the thought process. The dissonance becomes emotionally uncomfortable and builds over time until a "solution" is reached, a compromise in thought and belief. I believe people can influence or intimidate others into seeing their point of view, when that happens an individual will attempt to reduce the dissonance; the fact that their sources of information don't match when compared.

Stockholm syndrome and cognitive dissonance develop on an *involuntary* basis and this aligns up with my theory that Primary Emotional Caregivers are *not aware* of the effects they may be having on their children. (The child is not aware either). Both theories develop to survive a threatening, controlling situation or relationship and I propose it is the same foundational dynamic taking place within the families of homosexuals. "The more dysfunctional a situation is the more dysfunctional our adaptation and thoughts to survive." (Carver)

I was recently rereading the book titled, Facing Codependence, by Pia Melody, and although she did not say this, I am drawing the conclusion that what we may be seeing in the relationships between mothers and gay children is a unique manifestation of a particular type of codependent relationship. This is evidenced by each individual receiving what they need on an unspoken emotional level, which may be motivated by fear of loss of some sort. The unspoken message is," Don't be the gender of your birth," and the child's response is, "I won't be, but don't abandon or reject me."

These three relationship dynamics really show the potential for one human being to alter the mindset and perceptions of another person, even unknowingly. The thoughts that we have about our own physiology and self-awareness can be contradicted by a parent and then the child can add new cognitions, thoughts and attitudes, to reduce the stress felt between two points of view. The child, in my opinion, perceives their gender and behavior is the issue, so they adapt with new thinking and new behaviors. The rejection that the child perceives doesn't necessarily have to be hostile or openly aggressive, but I do believe certain behaviors are firmly unwelcomed and that opposite behaviors are somehow rewarded or encouraged.

5

CHAPTER FIVE

Research

I have read several theorists' works and how they believe that homosexuality occurs and I have observed that none of them have discussed the ideas that I propose here. Some have conducted studies that seem to parallel it and that in and of itself has caused an almost tracing affect around this theory and given it its own shape so to speak. These other studies have lightly touched on what I address here, but no one is addressing family dynamics in the same manner.

There are a few studies which have made some statements that would align with this theory but they are only puzzle pieces of a much larger picture. I am going to share some of that information and further demonstrate my view of transgenderism. I believe this theory of Gender Rejection/ Gender Replacement© has strong validity. This theory may not apply to every situation but it can be a template or yard stick to measure and assess an individual who may be confronted with this issue and you may be able to share this book with them or use it yourself or for your child.

Regarding research of homosexuality, there is not been too much in the last few decades and that in and of itself is significant. One reason there is little research of late is that in early 70's, the authors of the DSM III (The Diagnostic and Statistical Manual, which counselors, psychologist and psychiatrist use to diagnose mental disorders), were having their convention in San Francisco and a group of homosexuals disrupted the event and latter demanded the authors to take homosexuality, as a mental disorder, out of the manual.

The activists disrupted the conference by interrupting speakers and shouting down and ridiculing psychiatrists who viewed homosexuality as a mental disorder. In 1971, gay rights activist Frank Kameny worked with the Gay

Liberation Front collective to demonstrate against the APA's convention. Bayer (1973)

So from that time forward it was taken "off the books" and the issue of homosexuality as a psychological disorder has been virtually ignored. Although much research regarding homosexuality had come to a standstill, there were some earlier studies. If you go back before 1973 you can see some research was conducted that aids in supporting this theory of Gender Rejection / Gender Replacement. I will bullet point the studies here.

- Psychiatrists Byne and Parsons, writing in Archives of General Psychiatry, state that "it seems reasonable to suggest that the stage for future sexual orientation may be set by experiences during early development, perhaps the first 4 years of life."

- Another focus of researchers has been how the *personality traits of the parents* may contribute to same-sex attraction. Theories about how a child's relationship with his or her parents can affect homosexual feelings can be traced in the psychiatric literature going back nearly <u>a century</u>: Marvin Seigleman, (1974)

{At this point it would be good to reference the 3 ego states of Transactional Analysis. Briefly, it states we have 3 ego states: The Parent, The Adult and The Child within each of us. Communication, verbal and non-verbal, can emanate from any or all ego states from one individual to any or all ego states in another individual. The ego state where we mostly carry pain, is in the child ego state. More on this later}

In the book, <u>Games Alcoholics Play,</u> by Claude Steiner, Ph.D., He states on page 56, regarding an interaction between two parents and a child, … "while one homosexual's mother enjoined him not to be a man, the parent ego states of both parents demanded that he be a man." So here in lies a nonverbal, dual message, from the mother.

Steiner states that, in the mother, one ego state is doing the rejecting. This is why I believe the rejection is hard to detect because it is subconscious for both the mother and the child and it appears to be operating in the child ego state of the mother. I propose that the wounded child ego state of the mother may be unknowingly directing emotional vibes or statements toward their child and then the confusion and pain gets compartmentalized into the child ego state of the child. For both of them, the process is taking place in the subconscious. The mom is sending vibes (through non-verbal cues) or acting out toward the child and the child does not have the cognitive ability to discern what is going on so it "feels" the environment and in this way, it receives its prompts for behavior and thought. There may be other modeling behaviors at work but this appears to be the foundational issue. The child's behavior is reward based, so they down play their birth gender for the mother's (or primary emotional caregiver's) sake. The self-perception of the child, over time, moves from the child ego state and then solidifies in the adult ego state as their final self-perception.

On page 42 Steiner talks about, "…a male who has practiced a sort of depersonalized sex as a homosexual, which was an *adaptation* of his mother's injunctions." Again, I submit the idea that the entire behavior of a LGBT mind-set is adaptive behavior by the child to please his mother and avoid emotional abandonment or cognitive dissonance. The new found behavior is a coping mechanism for a stressful, emotionally indifferent or distancing situation; the possible loss of moms love and acceptance, which is *not* an option for a child.

- Several studies such as Freud's (1916) Archives of Sexual Behavior, describe the mothers of homosexuals as extremely loving and their fathers as retiring or absent.
- (Stekel 1930) noted strong dominant mothers and weak fathers. (I wonder if these mothers were somehow intimidating toward the child to compensate for their fear of men.)
- Terman and Miles (1936) found that mothers of homosexuals to be especially demonstrative, affectionate and emotional while fathers were typically unsympathetic, autocratic or frequently away from home.

These early studies suggest that the distance and coldness of the fathers is a potential cause for homosexuality but I suggest that the distance is evidence of a marital issue caused by men issues and that divorce or distance is an "off-shoot" symptom of the already underlying and manifesting problem within the marriage relationship.

- One study which begins to show the pattern that I am proposing is that of Dr. Irving Bieber. He said, "…The classical homosexual triangular pattern, in which the mother is close bonding with the son and is dominant and *minimizing* toward the husband, who is a detached father …Particularly a hostile-detached one." (Note the *minimizing* attitude observed in the mothers)

This scenario may be a bad marriage due to the husband and wife both having men and or women issues and the whole interaction gets played out in the family with the child's sexual orientation being acutely affected. The mother may be demonstrating how she feels about men in the marriage so the child may infer that being male is somehow bad. "Look how mom is treating dad, I may need to be different so as to not be treated "that way" or suffer some type of abandonment." I believe the observed, negative, male interactions of the mother, contributes to the child's Gender Replacement mind sets and behaviors.

- Bieber did a study comparing 106 homosexuals to 100 heterosexuals. Out of 106 homosexuals, <u>64</u> said that they wish they were heterosexual. (Almost two thirds.) One of the major hurdles for them to overcome to engage in heterosexual activity was they could not get past their anxieties and inhibitions.

I propose that if anxiety is the major issue, then their anxiety may be a result of the internal conflict that arises over the subconscious will of a parent (instilled in them) versus their own psychological and physiological drives. I am not proposing that these men are afraid of sex, but there may be an internal fear of the consequences of acting heterosexual, for example, "If I act too manly, this is going to cost me something in my relationship with my mother." Once again, these are feelings and thoughts that are deeply repressed in the child ego state because we are dealing with mind-sets that were imposed on a child at a very young age and these thoughts are barely distinguishable between those of the child and the expectations of the parent.

In several ways, this excerpt by Bieber adds to this theory. The article is listed in the reference section and I highly recommend reading it. Although the article does not have the same conclusions as my theory, after you read this book and his article, you will see things in a different light.

More studies

- In an Air Force study 30 out of 40 homosexual men reported the same mother/son relationship but no one had a close, warm and affectionate attachment to his father.
- In 1974 Marvin Siegelman confirmed Bieber and *more*: "The homosexuals, in contrast to heterosexuals reported their fathers to be more rejecting and less loving. The homosexuals also described their *mothers* as more rejecting and less loving,"

I propose that the dads were not around anymore because the marriages went bad to do men/women issues. If the mothers have men issues, and they negatively affect the marriage, then one can see how the mother might reject the son's gender as well.

Regarding one study conducted by Suftin, Ryan and Patterson (2007)

- "…We found that with parents, gender role attitudes were significantly associated with children's gender role attitudes; *Parental attitudes were a key variable*…. This finding is consistent with a variety of related results that point to the importance of <u>attitudes</u>, <u>behaviors</u>, and <u>relationships</u> within the family…"

- Social cognitive theory (Bussey and Bandura, 1999) suggests that parent attitudes about gender may be transmitted to children in a variety of ways, including modeling gender-typed appropriate behavior, reacting to children's gender-typed behavior, and directly instructing children as to what is appropriate.

- In 1996 Ray B. Evans of Lima Linda University School of Medicine wrote that "Bieber's data was based on psychoanalytic reconstruction of patient's early lives derived from the clinician's impressions during psychotherapy. Evans data, on the other hand, was based on Retrospective self-reports (memory) of how the client viewed their child hood."

"The results were remarkably similar in revealing more negative features in the backgrounds of homosexuals. Yet, Evans findings showed more detail; the mothers of the homosexuals were considered puritanical, *cold toward men*, insisted on being the center of the son's attention…made him her confidant, were seductive toward him, (My mom was not seductive toward me but she was sensual on an emotional level due to broken barriers from her sexual abuse) …allied with the son against the father (Men issues)…interfered with heterosexual activities during adolescence, discouraged masculine attitudes and encouraged feminine ones. (*Operant Conditioning* is clearly shown here, when he *acts less masculine* then he receives a nurturing reward and the cycle repeats itself.)

The relationship with the dads in this study is also very poor, it shows a distance and hatred and some fear of harm, but I theorize these thoughts and behaviors are copied and pasted from mom's attitude towards men. Even if dad is distant, hostile and autocratic, I do not believe that there is the same element of fear, shame or guilt which can be conveyed by the mother.

(My dad was around until I was 11 and we had enough healthy interaction so I had his behavior as a reference. Also, my mom did not bad mouth him or men often enough to cause me to rethink my gender.)

"Is there a *Contradiction?*"

First, we have studies that show mothers who are overly affectionate and indulging toward their sons and that seems to be a precursor to a LGBT mind set and now we see mothers who are distant, puritanical and cold…so which is it? It is both and here is how it works. First, you *have* to look at the *emotional motivations* of the mother and how they are expressed toward the child. Specifically, we need to look at both positive and negative reinforcement for behaviors. [This not to be confused with punishment which is a direct effect of undesired behavior, i.e. "little Johnny breaks his mother's vase after being told many times to not play ball in the house," so now he gets a paddling or a time-out because of *direct* disobedience.]

The first scenario is *positive reinforcement or Operant Conditioning,* which is the overly doting mother; here is how that works: Little Johnny comes inside after playing and he is filthy because he has been playing in the dirt with other boys, and the mother says something like this, "Oh Johnny, look at you, your clean clothes are now all dirty (vocalized shame and disapproval), I'll tell you what (happy voice filled with anticipation), why don't you get all cleaned up and put on your new white shoes, and clean shirt and shorts and I'll make you a nice bowl of vanilla ice cream and then we'll go shopping! Would you like that?" (She says with a big smiling face.) This is a positive reward for desired behaviors…stay clean and don't do what other boys do. Little Johnny is now *positively reinforced* with ice cream and a trip to the mall.

The second scenario is <u>negative reinforcement</u>. The way this operates is that you *take away a negative experience.* For example: Little Johnny comes in from playing and once again he is filthy. The mother is instantly cold, aloof and indifferent. She may look him up and down and scoff at how dirty he looks. He will pick up on this unwelcoming attitude and figure out why she is acting this way. He will go clean up and change and when he returns, she will be warmer and engaging. She may reward him with something tangible such as ice cream but what is really reinforcing his behavior to not be dirty, and not to be like the other boys, is the *removal* of her cold, indifferent attitude (the negative stimuli). He learns that in order to please her, and keep the emotional environment peaceful, he needs to comply with expectations. The underlying message is, don't be like the other boys.

As stated earlier in the Air Force study, if a father is not around, or is emotionally absent, and the male child is the mom's confidant, an inappropriate bonding can occur and this can precipitate an LGBT mindset. But again, although the mom embraces the child on one level, the male-ness is not encouraged and the child's masculinity is broken down systematically through their "coffee talks", shopping times...basically doing things together that the mom should be doing with a lady friend.

[I distinctly remember being happy when *any* of my mom's friends would come over because then I could "escape." I think because of my mom's broken emotional boundaries, due her sexual abuse, that there was a natural repulsion to her emotionally, because it was tainted with sexual issues, and this kept a type of wall between us.]

Although there is distance with the fathers 50 to 70 percent of the time in some of these studies, it is the Gender Rejection factor that is the basis of this book; the mother's attitude toward the child's gender is the precipitator and the father's attitude, again, may be a compounding factor.

As I mentioned earlier there was a movement to rid the subject of homosexuality from the arena of psychological study.

- Bayer, (1973) the American Psychiatric Association *removed* homosexuality from its list of mental disorders. That decision did not come as a result of new research. Ronald Bayer, author of the most exhaustive treatment of the 1973 decision, has described what actually happened:

'A furious egalitarianism that challenged every instance of authority had compelled psychiatric experts to negotiate the pathological status of homosexuality with homosexuals themselves. The result was not a conclusion based on an approximation of the scientific truth as dictated by reason, but was instead *an action demanded by the ideological temper of the times.*'

Prior to 1973 an extensive literature existed on the role of upbringing and experience in the development of homosexuality, yet one of the unfortunate effects of the APA decision was to largely stifle further research on the psychological origins of homosexuality.

- Daniel G. Brown put it well forty years ago -but his ringing call to action has gone unheeded...
  "It is surprising there has not been greater recognition of this relationship among the

various disciplines... investigations by; Terman and Miles some 30 years ago, the independent findings of a number of clinical and research workers, and the recent noteworthy contributions of West and Bieber, there is now strong evidence and considerable agreement as to family dynamics in the development of male homosexuality. It, in summary, would seem that the family pattern involving a combination of a dominating, overly intimate mother *plus* a detached, hostile or weak father is beyond doubt related to the development of male homosexuality. Beginning with the penetrating clinical insights of Freud 50 years ago. **There would seem to be no justification for waiting another 25 or 50 years to bring this information to the attention of those who deal with children. And there is no excuse for professional workers in the behavioral sciences to continue avoiding their responsibility to disseminate this**

knowledge and understanding as widely as possible."

It is extremely clear that there was and is an ongoing socio-political agenda to keep studies and awareness of homosexuality at bay. I think this is a tragedy. I believe that there are many people who would like to know why they think that they are gay. (And Bieber's study indicates that two thirds of them do.) I think the truth, whether it is this theory, or someone else's, should have ample opportunity for everyone to examine it and determine for themselves if it applies to them.

This event was 45 years ago. I think it is a sad situation because there are people who have struggled with this issue and maybe they did not have to. Due to a group of people, that stonewalled research, four decades of children may have grown up into this type of dysfunctional family. I believe truth is important because it is the "Truth that sets you free." (John 8:32)

I do not believe that homosexuality is a disorder, as in there is a psychological or physiological *problem*, so to speak, but I do believe it is mind set, a pathology and an adaptive behavior due to rejection.

When I was in high school there was a student there and everyone knew he was gay. Charlie was likeable and never caused any problems. He would unabashedly run and slide down the halls in his white leather loafers; he would lisp and his bodily movements were exaggerated; he was the iconic gay male. They killed Charlie. Two years after graduation a couple of guys beat him up and threw him off of a bridge. That happened in 1983. I wonder what would have happened if, ten years earlier, studies had continued and someone presented this theory or perhaps another, that addressed a cause of homosexuality? I wonder how many "Charlies", and society as a whole, might have been reached with understanding, rather than let this issue continue on, un-researched and ill-defined.

Erikson

Erik Erikson's developmental stages line up well with my theory and they add an additional piece of the puzzle. His early stages of development include 0-1-year-old which he calls the trust vs. mistrust phase. This is followed by 1-3 years old, which is characterized by autonomy vs. shame. And his third stage, which is ages 3-6, is initiative vs. guilt. If you put the three negative developments together you almost get my theory; *Mistrust* (a lack of security or bonding perhaps) *shame* for their gender and *guilt* for the way that they are. I propose that this is part of the foundational cause of homosexuality. Even the negative sides of Erikson's later stages show the same pattern continuing…Inferiority, Identity versus Role confusion and Isolation.

Memory

The following are a few studies on memory and they all consistently support the fact that most of our memories generally do not go back before the age of our third birthday. Carol Peterson, from Memorial University of

Newfoundland in Canada notes; "...14 to 16 -year olds first memories focused on incidents that had occurred when they were older than 4, on average."

- 'Elaine Reese, a colleague of Petersons, commented on the study and remarked, "You think about the emphasis on 0 to 3 in early education, but as adults we can't remember that period," she said. "It's one of those enigmas of science we'd like to understand."

- Dr. Peterson continues... "Children...do have the language skills, but often, by the time they grow up to be adults, those memories are gone."

- Fiona Jack and Harlene Hayne... suggest our earliest memories come from between the ages of three and four, some experts, Freud included, have suggested so-called infantile amnesia extends to the ages of five and six.

- John F. Kihlstrom, professor of psychology at the University of Wisconsin, and Judith M. Harackiewicz, surveyed 164 Harvard College students and 150 students at a high school and they found that the earliest memories were typically ones that occurred between the third and fourth birthdays.

I included memory research here because many transgender individuals state that they "have been this way as long as they can remember." I propose that certain relational dynamics have taken place within the family, of which, there are no current memories, only the lasting effects.

6

CHAPTER SIX

Cover up?

In 2009, Joseph J. Nicolosi, Ph.D., wrote a book entitled, Shame and Attachment Loss: *The Practical Work of Reparative Therapy*. His book is about reparative work that he has done in re-orienting homosexuals. He has had 2 decades of success, however, the American Psychological Association that evaluated his work was comprised of advocates for gay rights and it appears that their review was greatly biased according to Peter Kleponis, M.A. of the Institute of Marital Healing in West Conshohocken, PA.

They suggested that therapists tell their clients that re-orientation therapy is ineffective and that it is not possible.

It would seem that gays have infiltrated the very organizations that would analyze them and are promoting their own agenda. Although this book is not about those individuals, it should be pointed out that after several decades there is still a clear movement to bury potentially helpful and enlightening information on the topic of homosexuality.

In Nicolosi's findings, he talks about a domineering mother and a withdrawn father as we have read before in other studies and although all this seems to be a consistent find, I still maintain that there is another underlying issue. I believe the mother is domineering out of fear of men and her choice of a mate is indicative of unresolved men issues.

Nicolosi makes a statement about one young man in his article that almost says what this book is saying. Nicolosi states, "In order to be loved, he (the boy) must be someone he really is not." Nicolosi also talks about how the son takes his father's place emotionally (for the mother) and the son adopts a "good boy" persona rather than "being himself" and risking rejection.

I believe the son is altering his behavior to please his mother; otherwise it doesn't make sense for the son to do this unless there is some sort of stressor or re-warder involved.

Nicolosi uses the term, "double-bind," meaning the boy is receiving a dual message from the parents, "be good, but you are unlovable." I propose the son feels unlovable and that he must not be himself (gender wise) so he can appease the mother because of her "men issues."

Nicolosi clearly states that the boy is exhibiting adapting behavior within the family dynamic, however, what if the mother does have men issues? Then Nicolosi's conclusions would almost fit mine: *An altered persona, the son feels shame, he must change to be loved, and he becomes separated from his true self.*

7

CHAPTER SEVEN

Mother-Infant Bonding

There are two other studies that I would like to reference; the first one focuses on the bonding that takes place between a mother and her child and the other one studies the psychological evolution of a child in terms of physical evolution. (Darwin)

The first is *mother/infant bonding.* In a World Psychiatry Journal published in 2004, they discuss issues that certain women have regarding bonding with their newborn babies. In this issue they write about three levels of rejection toward babies by their mothers.

1. Ambivalence. 2. Rejection. 3. Anger.

Postpartum depression is a reality that some mothers go through; "she may express disappointment about her feelings toward her infant, she may have no feelings, feel estranged, distant, that it's not her baby or that she is babysitting for someone else."

My thought is, what if the basis of postpartum depression is a gender issue? What if there is no bonding because of unresolved issues in the mother's life? My future goal is to study these questions and topics at length. I wonder what results would be found if we tracked a group of 500 women, who have postpartum depression, and look at their child's behavior, as well as the mother's own gender opinions, 5 to 10 years later.

Again, some of this is a theory and you are among the first to hear it. I am simply asking the questions to generate thought and research. Obviously, more studies need to be done but the process needs to begin.

I had a photography business for many years and one year I did day care photography. I remember a few boys who had gelled hair and fake diamond earrings and who behaved in an effeminate way. I propose that the boys did not gel their own hair nor did they go to the mall alone to have their ears pierced. *Someone else dressed these 5-year-old children.* It is these types of parental influences that should be observed and evaluated as gender influencing or rejecting behaviors.

The second topic is Human Ethology. Ethology is concerned with the evolutionary significance of an animal's behavior in its natural environment. My intention will be to look at children in their homes during their first 5 years.

This article's study used ethology as a way of explaining observable phenomenon in babies that could not necessarily be explained by learning or other concepts. John Bowlby and Mary Ainsworth (1991) used ethology to explain aspects of infant-caretaker attachment theory. They state that, "...attachment has evolved because it promotes the survival of helpless infants."
Lorenz states that, "Certain fixed action patterns developed out of motivation for survival."

Bowlby also "...believes that humans spontaneously act to meet the demands of the environment. They are active participants who seek out a parent, food, or mate, etc."

This study basically looks at how adaptive behaviors produce an evolutionary effect. My perspective is a side bar. While they are looking at physiological changes caused by behavioral adaptations, I am looking at behavioral adaptions to physical and emotional environmental issues. They state that adaptations do exist. I am stating what the adaptive behavior is and to what the child is adapting to. I propose it is altered natural gender behaviors and mind sets to accommodate an undesirable emotionally (gender) rejecting environment.

The study goes on to say that "one can only understand the function of behavior by seeing how it specifically fits into the species natural environment in order to fulfill a specific need."

The methodology of this study could be used to observe the behaviors that I have mentioned. 1. Follow the subject in its natural environment. 2. See how different maternal behavior encourage emotional and mental "survival." ... (Acceptance/ rejection and nurture/ un-nurtured) 3. Determine the cause of certain child behaviors.

The focus of study needs to be on the true inner motivations, feelings, and attitudes of a mother toward both genders.

CHAPTER EIGHT

Illustrations

It was the Holy Spirit who first spoke this concept to me. One night while I was driving, He said, "Homosexuality isn't about rejection by the father, its rejection by the mother." Since then I have been able to line up this template to other homosexuals and their parents and see that it is easily observed once you know what to look for.

I should back up just a bit here though; homosexuality was something that I have observed since high school. Since then I have always known one or two individuals who were gay. The concept never really made sense to me though and

I have made note of different conversations and observations and one of the more obvious "red-flags" that I heard was something that a dad said in regard to his homosexual son. He said that while growing up he would invite Jimmy to go and do things together but Jimmy didn't want to go. This statement really stuck out to me because now I know, Jimmy was not trying to get closer to his father, he wanted to be closer to his mother. I remember thinking, "isn't that interesting, I wonder why he wouldn't want to be with his dad when he was younger if a dad's absence is the "supposed" missing element that initiates homosexual behavior" (My early deduction). If the "basis of homosexuality" is that there is a missing component in the father/ son relationship, one would think that the male child would be clamoring for the father's attention but in this case, and I believe most others too, the child is longing for something that the mother has withheld…gender approval. No wonder there is confusion stated by people who practice homosexuality. Their inner core self is at odds with itself…the individual may have the desire for the opposite sex but then there is another internal message of, "Don't," but it's the *why* that has created all the confusion...where did the message come from?

Over the years I have remembered statements from gay people such as, "I have been this way as long as I can remember" and "I was born this way." (That is why I included memory research in the last chapter) My daughter is 4 right now and she is amazing. She has a great vocabulary and a good sense of humor. She is a real person in every way, but I know in 10 years she will not remember our relationship the way it is today. She won't remember things we did or places we went to or the conversations that we had. Most people's memories only go back to about the ages of 3 to 5 and the memories are fleeting at best. I say this to say that moments and details of disapproval, that begin when kids are that young, are not necessarily things that are remembered when they get older. A child can be taught something at a very young age and not remember *when* they learned it so it is easy to see why someone may believe that something *always was* when in fact it *was not*.

This theory of Gender Rejection is apparent in the lives of some celebrities. Because they live in "glass houses," it is easy to observe them. I won't mention their names here but you can see headlines in the tabloids that talk about mothers and daughters and I think if you line up this theory with their lives you can see how this idea of Gender Rejection may apply. A mom's subconscious attitudes towards a gender can manifest in many different ways such as jealously, competition or indifference.

What can be confusing about this theory of Gender Rejection is that the child is not completely rejected; only their gender is. On one hand there can appear to be a close relationship between the mother and child, like Freud's client and her mother, but under the surface there can be quiet hatred, fear, disdain, jealousy or competition toward the gender of the child. The child could feel that all of them is being rejected but in reality, it is only one aspect that is being targeted by the parent and that may be why we see one area of the child's life so altered.

To test this theory all you have to do is look at the mother's true attitude toward each gender and also look at the mom's relationship with her own mother and father.

Again, this is a generational dynamic issue. Knowing your family's true history can really help fill in the gaps to see if this theory relates to your family. If there is a history of some type of abuse then you may see this theory exhibited.

CHAPTER NINE

Identity

When a person is confused about who they are, their identity needs to be adjusted and God can do that. It's important to look at *how* you were created ... male or female. It is important to start with that. I know some people have probably been searching for some deeper hidden cause of homosexuality but if you really consider what I am sharing here I think you will start to see some puzzle pieces come together in your life.

You are <u>more than acceptable</u> just the way you were born. You do not have to change. Your Primary Emotional

Caregiver is the individual that needs to change. It is *their* perspective of your gender that was imposed on you. You were given biased, incorrect information and an opinion that had nothing to do with you as a person. An opinion was imposed on you by someone who was wounded or abused by someone of a particular gender and therefore they may have found it too difficult to nurture the gender that you were created with.

This being said, the foundational stones that were laid to form your identity were stones of incorrect information. These inadvertent attitudes were based on a wounded perception of what a man or woman is. These stones that make up your foundational identity need to be replaced, one by one, with words of truth, God's word, and as you do this, as you choose to believe what God says about you, you will begin to have clarity and eventually you will have the wholeness, fulfillment, completion and acceptance that you have been longing for.

The wholeness lies in the acceptance of how you were created. It is a brave step to begin this process but when you can accept that God loves you, then you can begin to make statements in your mind toward the words, thoughts and mind-sets that were imposed on you. "I am fearfully and wonderfully made..." Psalm 139:14

Begin to say these words of truth and affirmation in your own mind and then start to say it out loud in the privacy of your own home or in your car and watch what happens to your understanding of yourself. Eventually you may have the opportunity to say something to the person who imposed their Gender Rejection onto you, if not, that is ok, you can do it for yourself and God will be with you to help you the whole way. This new knowledge and practice will begin the restoration process and it will eventually set you free. This process may sound simplistic but it is these incremental steps that will untie the "lie knots" in your mind-sets; what you have believed about yourself. Simply take one step at a time. The initial cause of your current mindset was incremental, you are tracing the steps backwards now, "reverse engineering" if you will.

As a gay person you may have felt an increasing confidence as you began to embrace and identify with an open gay life-style due to relaxing societal norms and now you may have the thought that leaving the gay life-style could leave you feeling at a loss, but I want to encourage you that God will create a new identity in you and that lost feeling will subside. Your new identity is how you were truly created combined with your relationship with God and who He says you are. God will help you reconstruct your "self" with foundational words of truth. Theses stones of truth will make up your new foundation and Jesus is the corner stone upon which you can build. He is the Way, the *Truth* and the Life. (John 14:6)

Your self-perception was distorted by one person, let Truth re-orient you back to how you were created. "In the beginning… God created them male and female" (Genesis 1:27)

Just because one person rejected a part of you does not mean that you have to also.

10

CHAPTER TEN

Now What?

"Ok Scott, I have read your theory and I see how it applies to my life, now what do I do?" First, I would ask you to ask God for guidance and understanding on how to relate to your mom and to anyone whom you may be in a relationship with now. We are talking about going back to the foundation of what has been built in your life and we are replacing it brick by brick with new stones of truth and facts about who you are.

Please do not use this new understanding to rail against anyone. Understand that everyone carries pain and unfortunately, we pass it on to the next generation most of the time. I honestly believe that moms are *not* aware that they are doing this, nor are practicing homosexuals misleading others as to why they are acting the way that they do.

Because God is our creator, I encourage you today to begin a consistent prayer life, nothing fancy, just open up lines of communication with God and begin to ask him to systematically replace wrong thinking, feelings, and mindsets with truth and facts. Ask Him to heal all the pain in your heart and mind and to bring clarity to all the issues of your life. Remember...God is a perfect Dad and He knows exactly how to mend our broken hearts. He knows how to communicate truth to us. He has not and will not reject you! He loves you and He will renew you.

My prayer for everyone reading this is that the Truth will set you free, (John 8:32) free to be who God made you to be, as well as equip you to help others.

I recommend counseling to help you sort through the thoughts and emotions that you will encounter as you address this issue in your life.

(One of the biggest keys to unlocking the bondage that has occurred, because of generational abuse and ensuing rejection, is forgiveness. You can ask God for a heart of forgiveness and He will help you. There may be times where it will seem impossible but ask Him and let Him work on your heart and mind.)

11

CHAPTER ELEVEN

Healing

If this theory seems to fit your life, how you proceed from this point forward is extremely important. First, it would be inappropriate and potentially damaging to confront your Primary Emotional Caregiver without really processing this information for yourself first. The repair and reintegration of your true sexual identity is delicate and may take some time. Use wisdom when and if you decide to discuss this issue with a parent.

Spending time with God in prayer and reading His word is the best thing to do to begin. This is a foundational stone in your rebuilding. There is no need to rush the process, simply take one day at a time and let God work on the inside.

If you are currently with a partner just be open with them about this new information and if possible, take this walk together. God is about extending love and building healthy relationships.

Jesus was despised and rejected; He knows your pain. A lot of people had some very different thoughts about who He was. Some thought He was demon possessed; nothing could be further from the truth. Jesus connected with humanity through our pain, suffering and rejection so that we can connect with God's acceptance, love and righteousness. He knows where you are coming from and now, He wants you to know where He is coming from.

Spend time reading the Psalms, Proverbs, the Book of John, Acts and all the smaller letters of the New Testament and this will help you see who God is and who you are and you will also learn about the new life that He has for you to live.

12

CHAPTER TWELVE

A Message to Moms

If this theory of Gender Rejection applies to your
relationship with your son or daughter then you may be
experiencing some extreme emotions right now and that is
normal. To actually face the fact that you may have
inadvertently "pushed" your child toward homosexuality,
because of your unresolved issues and unforgiveness with
men or women, is a big pill to swallow. The next step is
honesty and humility with God, yourself and your child.
Because this issue is so complex, and decades may have
gone by, you may be thinking, "Where do I even start?"

My suggestion is to be honest about your feelings toward those that hurt YOU first. I would encourage counseling to help you resolve the pain in your own life and then turn toward your child and help them to understand what may have taken place in your relationship with them.

The foundational stones in your child's life were laid one at a time; Stones of rejection, misinformation, neglect or unkind comments. Whatever it may be, these stones need to be replaced with statements of love, nurturing, honesty and humility. A new foundation of words of affirmation needs to be laid for their lives; A foundation of truth of who they really are.

If your child was born male then that's indicative of what they were supposed to be. In the case of homosexuality, this identity is buried or discarded but it is the true identity. Help your child to be restored with words of truth and affirmation about how they were created. If you are still struggling with your own personal issues and you cannot accept your child as they were born, then at least admit it and tell them that the issue is *yours* and *not* theirs. Our children can become the accidental victims of issues that are not their own and they deserve to know the truth.

Again, I encourage everyone who is involved to seek good counsel and take the process one step at a time, asking God to guide you every day and He will.

If this theory does apply to your life, I strongly recommend adjusting all attitude, speech and behaviors toward your child. The younger the child is the better the chance for a more seamless transition back to what they were supposed to be…how they were created. If you realize that you may have caused this issue in their life, then start speaking and acting in accordance with truth and be consistent and approving in your speech and actions and your child will respond. Love covers a multitude of sins. (1 Peter 4:8)

Let your kids feel your love and acceptance today.

Side Note...Early Development

Dr. Spock indicates that children, when they are young, will "fall in love" with the opposite parent. This is a formative process in a young child's life. I do not believe that the rejection in this season of a daughter's life by her dad has the same lasting impact as the son who goes through the infatuation stage as the mother. I say this because the fathers are not the Primary Emotional Caregiver, the emotional survival person of children in general. The need for life giving elements such as clothing, food, time, attention, nurturing and love, usually come from the mother and I believe the fear of losing her love and approval are the motivating factor that influences a child's behavior. Even if a mother is rejecting of her son during this time, it is not the deciding factor, rather it is incremental rejection over time that shape the child's self-perception.

Dr. James Dobson has written many books on raising children that you may find helpful.

13

CHAPTER THIRTEEN

Random thoughts

The issue at hand is emotional rejection of the gender of a child by the Primary Emotional Caregiver which is precipitated by unresolved gender issues. It is rejection of a gender, by the mother because of fear, which leads to fear of abandonment by the child, which causes a radical change in thinking, self-perception and ultimately behavior. The child comes into agreement with the parent's wishes so that they can be loved, nurtured and accepted; it is as basic as that. They continue to live out a role, whether in thought or action, because this is the course that they were set on. It is a mindset that has caused this situation and it is a new mindset that can bring someone out of it. This issue really does remind me of the Stockholm syndrome. The captive empathizes with the kidnappers and adapts to their thinking and it is based on fear and survival instincts. The fear is abandonment and isolation or fear of unknown repercussions. The captive takes on the role that keeps them alive. Kids are not kidnapped per-se but where else can they go? They are in a situation that they do not even understand, let alone can begin to undo.

This theory may not fit all situations. There are cases of sexual assault, molestations, incest, etc., that can be contributing factors to the re-orienting of a child's sexual identity, however, acknowledging one's gender is still the truth and you can regain your true sexual identity.

Sexual experiences are powerful and they can leave a lasting "impression" so to speak, especially on a child. The God that created the universe and you and I, can heal those early traumatic memories and give you a fresh perspective and a new life in Him. We are His creation and we are still "under warranty." If we return to Him, He is more than willing able to address any issue in our lives.

Homosexuality has become the focal point of topic and debate but it is not the issue. The motive is what no one is seeing or understanding, and I suggest not even the individuals themselves know. The attention is misdirected from the source of the behavior because the child was sent in that direction a long time ago.

As a society our attention is on the behavior but we have only been speculating about the cause and in some cases ignoring data or simply doing no research at all due to societal pressures. When you take this theory, this yard stick, and you begin to measure relationships and behaviors, then I believe that you will observe gender dysphoria issues in a new light.

The devil's greatest tactic is to send a wound of some sort, an assault, a violation, an abuse or abandonment, the list goes on, and in that wound in one's heart he sows a seed of lies. For example; a woman gets raped and the lie is, 'I'm unclean or dirty." A girl gets sexually abused and the lie is "I'm worthless." A child gets rejected by a parent... "I'm no good." When we are abused, un-nurtured, ignored or wounded in any way, we will begin to believe a lie about ourselves and unfortunately it can take time to re-write that event, "but with God, all things are possible." (Mark 10:27)

14

CHAPTER FOURTEEN

Jesus and You, a Love Story.

Jesus loves <u>you</u>!!

That may seem like a trite statement, perhaps it has been over used and the strength and sincerity of it has faded, but if you can believe it one more time and really let God into your heart and life and ask Him to start revealing truth to you, I know you won't be disappointed.

The Bible says that the Devil comes to steal, kill and destroy but I (Jesus) have come that you might have life and have it more abundantly. (John 10:10)

"For I know the thoughts that I think toward you,
saith the LORD, thoughts of <u>peace</u>, and not of evil,
to give you an expected end." (Jeremiah 29:11)

Many people think that God has or will reject them for one
reason or another or because their sin is too great but that
simply is not true. Many people reject God *first* because
they believe that He will ultimately reject them, again, I say
it's not true. God made provision for salvation for us long
before we needed it. (Romans 5:8) He made a way of
salvation that more than takes care of our wrong doings.
His plan takes care of our very sin nature. He has
thoroughly dealt with our issues before we ever became
aware them. Now that we are aware of them many times
we run from Him, we hide, we deny, we rebel, we
rationalize, we do everything before we come to the
realization that he actually loves us and that He has more
than paid the price for our transgressions...*more* than paid
for them. All we have to do is acknowledge that we need
his salvation and *accept* His provision of forgiveness and
reconciliation; His sacrifice on the cross, for ourselves and
our sins personally, and then He says, "as far as the east is

from the west He has separated us from our sins." (Psalm 103:12)

Sin is weighty, it needs to be atoned for, it is a spiritual law; everyone must pay. However, God said that people can *never* pay the price; they do not have the ability to no matter what they do, so I will send a perfect sacrifice, Jesus, the perfect atonement. He is the Lamb of God that was slain for the sins of the world, once and for ALL. (John 1:29)

God is more concerned with you as a wounded and rejected person than He is with any sin that you may have committed. But He has graciously and mercifully dealt with both issues.

There is therefore now *no condemnation* to them which are in Christ Jesus, who walk not after the flesh, but after the Spirit. (Romans 8:1) If we turn toward God and allow the Holy Spirit to assist us in our Christian walk, though we may stumble, He will uphold us. (Isaiah 41:10) He knows we won't get it right every time and that we will have to start over occasionally, but as long as we don't turn away from

Him, we will discover that His arm is always stretched out toward us to lift us up to go again.

God says we are created in His own image…this is our new identity, "in the image of God created he him; <u>male and female</u> created he them". (Genesis 1:27) He says that there is nothing that can separate us from the love of God. He is our Dad and His arms are stretched out and opened wide to receive you *today*!

People are looking for freedom and whom the Son sets free is free indeed! (John 8:36)

Will you try again today and give your life to Jesus and ask Him for new life, eternal life? If so, please pray this simple prayer and begin a new and fresh walk with God today.

> "Dear Father, I come before you now, I don't even know how to start or what to say exactly, but I believe and accept that you paid the price for my sins with the atoning sacrifice of Jesus' shed blood on the cross. Please cleanse me from all unrighteousness and heal my life. Jesus, please be my Lord and Savior beginning now. Help me to know

you and to know who I am. Thank you for
eternal life, healing and restoration, Amen."

15

CHAPTER FIFTEEN

The Beach Road

We did not have a lot of money when I was growing up so when we needed to get out the house, we would often just take a drive down the beach road. We would start in Rye, and then drive up the coast through New Castle and then through downtown Portsmouth. It was always a nice ride and I loved to go by the beach no matter what time of year it was. We would often park near Wallis Sands and get out of the car and walk on the rocks and watch the waves break down below. During the summer I would fish and snorkel there.

One such day I was there with my mother and this was the second time she had asked me if I was gay and now, I know why. We were having an argument about something, nothing too heated but a few issues came up and I can now reflect on that day differently. She said to me, "I never touched you you know," (meaning sexually). I wasn't sure if she had or not but I didn't think about it too much) Then she said, "The doctors said I was too sensual." (Symptoms of her sexual abuse). Her concern was that because she was sexually abused and because it had affected her, that she may have inadvertently affected me with her "sensuality." (Those who have been sexually abused tend to have poor walls and boundaries in the realm of their sexuality so their issues tend to be self-evident.)

In retrospect I understand what she had been trying to say. (Even as I began to write this chapter) She knew she was "too sensual" and she thought that even though she had never touched me, she thought she might have caused me to be gay somehow and *that* was her fearful concern that I had been sensing during those years…that she had somehow influenced me with her issues. I think pride and awkwardness kept her from asking so she would just bark the question at me. She was concerned that her past might have affected my life, to somehow cause homosexuality, but it hadn't. It is clear to me now that she was aware of her possible influence on me, however, she had had enough self-awareness that she watched her words and actions and there were only traces of her internal conflicts that were directed towards men. Like I said before, ninety eight percent of the time she was a good and caring mom. Her main concern was to not perpetuate the sexual abuse and in doing that she did not taint my sexual identity, which she easily could have influenced due to her fear and mistrust of men. I don't think she was aware of the cause and effect of a transgender mindset that I have illustrated here but she was cautious and inadvertently did not have a gender rejecting attitude toward me.

Because she confronted the topic and cleared the air, we were able to move past our issues. This was a brave step on her part and she did it. It was awkward though, I was in my twenties at that point, but she brought it up and it made a significant difference in our relationship.

My mom is gone now. I wish she had been around longer, I could have used some more parenting advice, especially when it comes to finding things for my kids to do. Like I mentioned before, she was very creative and she could brighten up a rainy day with some kind of indoor activity. I also wish we could have talked about my life some more and perhaps hers too.

Reconciliation is so important. It can be messy but it is so essential. I encourage you to do what you can to find reconciliation in your relationships. It can really help bring a fresh start to everyone's life.

16

CHAPTER SIXTEEN

Conclusion

I wrote this book for several reasons. First, I wanted to share the information that I have discovered with the hope of bringing answers to help resolve conflicts within a person's heart, mind and soul about who they are.

Second, I wanted to help lay a new foundation and build a bridge to those who feel broken and isolated. There may be a social movement to keep knowledge of this topic hidden, however, I firmly believe everyone needs to hear the truth.

We are all born with a sin nature; a propensity to sin. No sin is greater that another. In a spiritual sense, we are all born behind enemy lines but God the Father has made a way through His Son Jesus to draw us out and reconcile us back to himself. Will you say yes to Him today? I hope that you do. He is reaching out to you, take a hold of His promises of a new life by believing and accepting Him today and receive a fresh start, a new life and yes, it is possible.

It does not take a village to raise a child, it takes two mature and committed parents, a mom and a dad, who are wise and loving toward their children. Families are the building blocks for society, if the family unit breaks down, so will society. I pray for the healing of families across the United States and around the world. What we need is restoration.

I hope this book has helped you to better understand how subconscious thoughts and emotions can be transferred within a family group. The Bible talks about "a root of bitterness springing up and defiling many." (Hebrews 12:15) We *must* be healed of our past pain so that we don't pass on the effects of it to our children.

The Beginning.

Psalm 104:2-14

"Who forgiveth all thine iniquities; who healeth all thy diseases; Who redeemeth thy life from destruction; who crowneth thee with lovingkindness and tender mercies; Who satisfieth thy mouth with good things; so that thy youth is renewed like the eagle's. The LORD executeth righteousness and judgment for all that are oppressed. The LORD is merciful and gracious, slow to anger, and plenteous in mercy. He will not always chide: neither will he keep his anger forever. He hath not dealt with us after our sins; nor rewarded us according to our iniquities. For as the heaven is high above the earth, so great is his mercy toward them that fear him. As far as the east is from the west, so far hath he removed our transgressions from us. Like as a father pitieth his children, so the LORD pitieth them that fear him. For he knoweth our frame; he remembereth that we are dust."

References

Bayer, Ronald, (1973) *Homosexuality and American Psychiatry: The Politics of Diagnosis* (Princeton, Summary of findings regarding the developmental causes of homosexuality

Bieber, Irving, MD. (1965): *Homosexuality: A Psychoanalytical Study* (New York: Vintage Books, 1962), 172 College Students," *Genetic Psychology Monographs*, 71 302–03.

Bieber, Irving, MD. *(1976) A Discussion:* "*Homosexuality: The Ethical Challenge*" Journal of Consulting Clinical Psychology 19/6 Vol. 44 No. 2 163-166

Boyles, Salynn. (2011) *When Do Kids Form First Memories?* WebMD Health News. Reviewed by Laura J. Martin, MD.

Brown, Daniel G., (Sept. 1963/1987) "*Homosexuality and Family Dynamics*," Bulletin of the Menninger Clinic. 27 (5):232 NJ Princeton University Press, 3. 27 (5): 229.

Carver, Joseph, M. Ph.D. (2004) *Love and Stockholm syndrome: The Mystery of Loving an Abuser*. Counseling Resource.

Evans, Ray B. (April 1969) *"Childhood Parental Relationships of Homosexual Men,"* Journal of Counseling and Clinical Psychology, 33 129, 133.

Freud, Sigmund (1920) Umber die Psychogenese eines Falles von weilblicher Homosexualtat. Internationale Seitschrift fur Psychoanalyze. VI, 1920, pp. 1024; GW, XII, pp271-302; *The psychogenesis of a case of homosexuality in a woman.* SE, 18 145-172.

Jack, F. & Hayne, H. (In Press). *Eliciting adults' earliest memories: Does it matter how we ask the question?*
Kihlstrom, J.F., & Harackiewicz, J.M. (1982). *The earliest recollection: A new survey.* Journal of Personality, 50, 134-148

Kleponis, Peter C., M.A., L.P.C. (2010) Book Reviews Downers Grove, IL: Inter Varsity Press, 2009. 474 pages.

Klier, Claudia, Muzik, Maria (2004) *Mother-infant bonding disorders and use of Parental Bonding Questionnaire in clinical practice.* World Psychiatry
June 3 (2):102-103.

Nicolosi, Joseph, J. Ph.D., (2009) *Shame and Attachment Loss: The Practical Work of Reparative Therapy.*

O'Connor, P. J., (May 1964) *"Aetiological Factors in Homosexuality as Seen in Royal Air Force Psychiatric Practice,"* "British Journal of Psychiatry, 110: 384–85.

Patterson Charlotte J. (2007) Published online: 15 December. Springer Science Business Media, LLC

Peterson, C. (2011). *Children's memory reports over time: Getting both better and worse.* Journal of Experimental Child Psychology, 109,275-293

Siegelman, Marvin (1974) "*Parental Background of Male Homosexuals and Heterosexuals,* "*Archives of Sexual Behavior*, 3 3-4. Homosexual problems.'"

Spock, Benjamin (1985) *Dr. Spock's Baby and Child Care.* Pocket Books, Simon and Schuster. NY, NY.

Sutfin, Erin L. and Megan, Fulcher & Ryan P. Bowles (2007): How Lesbian and Heterosexual Parents Convey Attitudes Published online: 15 December 2007
Springer Science + Business Media, LLC

Tinbergen, Eibl-Eibesfeldt- (1963) The *book Human Ethology* "On Aims of Methods of Ethology"

notes

www.ingramcontent.com/pod-product-compliance
Lightning Source LLC
Chambersburg PA
CBHW072315290526
45794CB00002B/673